1

Printed in the United States of America

First Printing, 2020

ISBN 978-1-71602-677-5

Lulu Press, Inc.
627 Davis Drive Suite 300

Morrisville, NC 27560

www.lulu.com

ISBN 978-1-71602-677-5

Dialogue From Within

Exploring Self Love and Acceptance Through Poetry

Renee Roley

Thank you Boss

1) My Breasts 1/12/19
2) I Have Courage 1/19/19
3) Self Love 1/26/19
4) Bravery 2/2/19
5) Forged 2/9/19
6) Cobwebs Clearing 2/16/19
7) Ich Liebe Sie 2/23/19
8) From / To 3/2/19
9) How Was I Strong This Week? 3/9/19
10) It's Behind Me Now 3/16/19
11) Have I Done Enough? 3/23/19
12) If / Then 3/30/19
13) Gulping Galaxies 4/6/19
14) i make 4/13/19
15) My Hair 4/20/19
16) Gender Fluid and Me 4/27/19
17) Reframing Sex 5/4/19
18) The Two Dots the "I" 5/11/19
19) An Attempt Reframed 5/18/19
20) R and Three Sides 5/25/19
21) Breath 6/1/19
22) I See Me 6/8/19
23) Center 6/15/19
24) I Cannot Find My Words 6/22/19
25) Feelings 6/29/19
26) I Am Worthy 7/6/19
27) ? 7/13/19
28) Reframing Motherhood 7/20/19
29) Celebrating Sissy 7/27/19
30) Why Try 8/3/19
31) Why Not Try 8/10/19

5

1.
Protruding gently
      They are soft
Growing slowly
      They are tender
Each inhale
      They rise
Each exhale
      They fall
They exist
      But more in my mind
They exist
      But are barren and dry
When I need them most
      They are comforting
When I mother myself
      They are nurturing
I love my breasts
      And want more of them
I love my breasts
      And want to share them

2.
I take a breath as my pulse heightens
Reminding myself to draw my chest back
Square my shoulders and lengthen my spine
      I have courage
I feel the fit of the jeans against my smooth skin
Pink nails, peach shoes, pink tank hidden underneath

As the balance of my wardrobe is more her than him
        I have courage
I see the eyes and recognize the recoil body shift
Like a mascot at a sporting event
In this city of twenty thousand...I don't fit
        I have courage
In shame I find myself walking against the wall
Hiding my hands and shielding my gaze
Constantly I remind myself to stand tall
        I have courage
Daily as I work in the belly of the beast
I draw on every ounce of strength
To remain in my power as I speak
        I have courage
What is courage if it is easy?
        What is courage if there is no risk?
                What is courage if I am not leading?
I have courage
        I have courage
                I ... am courage

3.
Pillows piled for my head
While another is left on the bed
        i
The door is locked and the lights are low
I leave it lie, soft and alone
        Il
I tease my mind and stroke my soul
Shame melts away as the lust rolls
        I lo
It rises and grows, hard and erect

It feels good in my hand smooth with Wet
        I lov
Responding naturally I feel the pleasure
No urgency, beautifully no pressure
        I love
The scars tickle my skin
For once ... I don't cringe
        I love m
Feeling its length up and down
Grateful for its rebound
        I love my
Fast or slow, hard or soft
It simply remains aloft
        I love my p
Through the portals of my kink
Joyfully I don't need to think
        I love my pe
Stroking and squeezing the head
Teasing myself too and from the edge
        I love my pen
I cum when I want, I cum how I want
With ease it spurts without any haunt
        I love my peni
Intimacy to myself is mine to give over
As I realize I am my own best lover
        I love my penis

4.
Walking that half mile
Once filled me with dread
Facing known danger
I thought I'd end up dead

I often walk it in my mind
Gaining strength and power
That brave little child
Forever refusing to cower

I owe a lot to that little being
Who had strength beyond years
I am only now finally seeing
Bravery is tempered by tears

5.
Character is created through the heat of life
Stoked by others as the coal fires light

The steel of my spine smashed into a billet
Heated and formed with heavy equipment

Teachers, neighbors, family and friends
All held the hammer forming my ends

Each influencer adding their mark
Until I took over with my heart

Sneaking back into the forge each night
My little being reshaped me with might

A self that was forged by my younger soul
Heated and quenched and made whole

Hiding behind flaws through years of neglect
I have discovered, every inclusion is perfect

I love myself in these moments
When I can admire my accomplishments

I made it through the hottest of fires
My little child self-inspired

I celebrate my pits
      And dents
           And blemishes
Because I am sharp
      And strong
           Thanks to them

6.
The pathways are brightening
As my hands brush webs free
Who am I? is my reckoning
And I am beginning to see

Layers of tapes removing
As I find fascination in my being
Messages re-recording
As my center is clearing

I am powerfully impactful
Driven while also kind
Joyful and delightful
Always stretching my mind

As I really look inside
I am open to seeing
A successful life
Ever more so freeing

7.
im kalten Morgengrauen
wie die sonne einsickert
sie kommt durch
die Unebenheiten auf meiner Haut

Ich habe ein Mädchen drin
          wer sehnt sich gesehen zu werden
Ich möchte sie durchhalten
          und lass sie leben
Ich möchte sie anziehen
          und geh sie herum
in ihrer Haut leben
          stark und stolz sein

Ich bin ein Mädchen im Inneren
wenn ich mir erlaube
die Schande fallen lassen
und lass sie geliebt warden

weil sie sie versteckt hält
          wird unmöglich

halten sie privat
        beraubt die Welt...und mich
von ihrer inspirierten Seele
        und ihr sanftes Herz
Ich habe ein Mädchen drin
        Ich möchte mich als sie lieben

mein Mädchen im Inneren
es tut weh, eine Frau zu sein
Sie sehnt sich nur nach einer Sache
und das ist für mich, sie zu lieben

7a. Translation

In the chill of the dawn
As the sun seeps in
She comes through
The bumps on my skin

I have a girl inside
        Who aches to be seen
I want to hold her out
        And let her live
I want to dress her up
        And walk her around
To live in her skin
        Being strong and proud

I am a girl inside
If I allow myself
To drop the shame
And let her be loved

Because keeping her hidden
  Is becoming impossible
Keeping her private
  It deprives the world...and me
Of her inspired soul
  And her gentle heart
I have a girl inside
  I want to love me as her

My girl inside
Aches to be a woman
She longs for one thing only
And that's for me to love her

8.
from masculine to feminine
from too old to young
from silly to demure
from ugly to sexy
from Square to whole
from fat to lithe
from thick to desired
from cringeful to sensual
from inelegant to powerful
from laughable to happy

9.
I wore pink shoes to work
  When I wanted to fade Renee away
I asked for support with scissors in hand
  When I wanted Renee's hair shaved

I got on the phone with a loved one
    When I wanted Renee erased
I applied for ten more jobs
    When uncertainty was raised
I fed myself after throwing up
    When stress around the oasis peaked
I used my resources to sleep
    When my mind kept me awakened
I gently took myself home and snuggled into bed
    After I broke down while I worked
I left the photos of Renee on my phone
    Even while I wanted them deleted
I leaned into my global impact for Trans rights
    While my government proclaimed me diseased

I savored the power of Renee's influence
    When I am authentically her
        As I witnessed a coworker come out
            Inspired by the courage of her
                And be embraced by
        colleagues
                    As his fluidity
            unfurled

Perhaps strength means something different
    Beyond being physically empowered
        Perhaps strength is about vulnerability
            And a willingness to be supported
                Not only by loved ones
                    But especially ... by
            ... Renee

10.
His daughter, fidgeting and nervous
        Her own being now but his shadow lingering
                Her own intentions unknown but grasping
Myself, poised and kind
        Standing in the power of "I forgive"
                Standing in the power of perspective
His physical being gone
        Ashes in a vessel
                Ashes in the sea
My voice to her calm and final
        "I hold no resentment to your father"
                "I hold no resentment to Jack"
Everything that happened did happen
        What happened formed me
                What happened shaped me
Now I am free of the shackles
        I am free of the shame
                I am free of the pain
It is behind me now
        Not forgetting
                Not condoning
It is behind me now
        Pushing forward in peace
                Pushing forward in love
It is...behind me

11.
When I consider myself
        My life
                My loves
                        My passions

Like books on a shelf
　　From word
　　　　To sentence
　　　　　　To chapter
I am a powerfully effectual
　　Creating opportunity
　　　　By preparation
　　　　　　By planning
As I reflect on my time inside the burm
　　Transforming experiences
　　　　Being the example
　　　　　　Shoes for Obama
Including some misses
　　Urinal for all
　　　　Interview with an athlete
　　　　　　Acceptance of peers
Including some massives
　　Global protection for Trans workers
　　　　Approval for pronouns
　　　　　　My perspective on belonging

As my time here draws close
　　I am more powerful
　　　　I am more confident
　　　　　　I am more impactful

Than I ever could have imagined

12.
If in the constant barrage of resume declines
I can be resilient
If in the narrowing of job options

I can be resilien
If in the most abrupt rejection
I can be resilie
If Fetal in bed at 2pm on a Thursday
I can be resili
If in the most silent moments of ghosting
I can be resil
If in the gawking my being draws
I can be resi
If in the silence when I enter break room
I can be res
If in the Growing decline of co lunching
I can be re
If in the relentless pace of work load
I can be r
If in the loud cacophony of loneliness
I can be
If in the financial pressure of ownership
I can b
If in the deep everlasting loss of hardness
I can
If in the impermanence of home
I ca
If in the presence of my abuser
I c
If in the midst of the most violent dreams
I
If in the growing density of homework
    If in the experience of abandonment,
      Of physical abuse,
        Of sexual abuse

I can be resilient
Then ... Then ... Then
I can be resilient now

13.
Borders began fading
       Walls crumbled down

Consciousness increasing
       Opening formed in my crown

Floating turning to flying
       Through the expanse space
Flying becomes being
       Boundaries gone without trace

I gulped galaxies
       I gulped galaxies
           I gulped galaxies
With an insatiable appetite

Pinpoints of light exploding
       Inside of my eyes
Stars exploding
       Stars exploding
           Stars exploding
Sending me their might
Shame and judgment releasing
       Genders melted gloriously into one
As my being vibrates

I hold the expanse of the universe
As my physical body melts away
I am the expanse of the universe
As time disappears
As my body disappears
As distance disappears
I am all genders equally
I am all genders
I am gender
I am all
Power is limitless and safe
As I feel I am god
Enlightened with grace
As I feel I am god

My god is within me
My god is me
I am my god
Even as I move today
I remain the universe
I remain expansive
I am

14.
Sensual moments that provoke feels
Active times that break down walls
New approaches to old ideas
New approaches to new ideas
I ideate
I create
I make
Experiences

Luxurious and textured to touch
Functional and practical yet lush
Continually asking why not
Continually asking what if
I ideate
       I create
              I make
                     Objects
I step out visible on the ledge
Pushing and stretching every edge
Always looking for opportunities
Always generating opportunities
I ideate
       I create
              I make
                     Safety
Leaning always into curiosity
Learning unknowns then building
Constantly probing how
Constantly learning how
I ideate
       I create
              I make
                     Innovation
Too numerous to list
Too disparate to segment
I, Ron, am a maker
I, Renee, am a creator
I ideate
       I create
              I make
                     Myself

15.
The weight gently wafts over my skin
Soft and textured to the touch
Curls tight and long beyond my chin
Tangled and twisted sometimes a crutch

Born from a self realization
Born on the date of separation

It lengthens and thickens each passing day
Blessing me with a before unknown gift
Often a topic of conversation on airplanes
Comforting me like a nest as my gender shifts

Born from self acceptance
Born from self love

I flick my bangs to the side with my finger
Softly and gently the gesture
Feminine in movement I linger
Enjoying the female in my posture

Born with me but unknown
Born to me and has grown

It helps me feel soft and graceful like a girl
Standing tall in my multi faceted self
Feminine energy in each and every little curl
Celebrating my womanhood, myself

Born to me and forever shall be
Born with me gracefully

I love my hair
I love my hair
I love my hair

16.
Two different liquids, cold, unmoving, separated
Waiting to be warmed up, needing to be heated

It takes a decision, a recognition, an embrace
To reach toward and flick a switch to integrate

For my entire life, the light remained off
The two liquids suspended, together but not

I have always known they both exist inside
Both equally beautiful and unified

Out of fear, safety and shame they remained suspended
Until one year, one month, one day I finally relented

Consciously I looked inside and reached a decision
To turn my inner lamp on with deep compassion

The light from my soul glows with loving warmth
The two liquids melting, slowly shifting in form

I am reminded of how the universe informed me

I am all genders equally
I am all genders
I am gender
I am all

I am empowered to release shame and judgment calmly

The longer I live within myself and for myself
The more elegant the liquids dance and blend

Beautifully natural and with freedom of limitless range
The fluidity of my being I want to celebrate

Much like a lava lamp on a bookshelf
My genders have combined into one self

17.
I am gripped with a guttural shame
        Looking inward I softly hug myself
Hesitation holds me from the plane
        Reframing tapes from when I was twelve

"Women only want to be with a man if he can ejaculate"
People want to be with me because I am passionate
"No woman will ever want to be with you"
I attract intimacy and joy like a magnet

What is sex if it's not about erections
        I choose to embrace I am more than a spout
Scarcity with love is an old construct
        I hold space for myself to quench the drought

I will enter into the room with my power
Offering myself without hesitation
Releasing my insecurities like dust in the shower
Opening myself to love and connection

I choose to celebrate intimacy of others
      I choose to allow that for myself

I choose to honor the function of others without a cloud
      I choose to honor my own unique gifts as well

I release the fear of scarcity
I hold myself open for others
No more shields or self severity
I hold myself open without edits

I want to hold this truth without judgment
      That I am enough
I am enough today and tomorrow
      I don't need to be any other

I am enough as I am here right now
      I am enough
I am enough as I present myself
      I am enough
I am enough that I attract play
      I am enough
I am enough and I am not broken
      I am enough

18.
The two dots the i, which color will I choose
        For the first time ever, looking is the hard step
Reddish hues of dark purple, offset by pink
        For the first time ever, seeing them is the work
Opening myself inside, and diving deep with calm
        For the first time ever, I count them one to five
Down a line of bumps, like the row of islands
        For the first time ever, I touch each one
They belong on me, they belong to me
        For the first time ever, I invite them in me
A relief sweeps over, as I release the hold
        For the first time ever, I see their beauty
They are who I am, they are me
        For the first time ever, I value them
I feel them connected, directly to my heart
        For the first time ever, I am grateful for them
For the first time ever, I don't feel ashamed
        For the first time ever, I find their power
For the first time ever, they are mine now

I am thankful for my scars,
They have guided me through the stars

19.
The skin is healed and nearly clear
        1982 was a long time ago
Sitting in the green dodge dart
        I did it in a parking lot
Exacto knife was the chosen tool
        Used for the newspaper in school
Despair had reached the lowest

As my youth had been stolen
And while I did it that evening night
It didn't happen despite
The silence of my family
As the wound bled through bandage
Was another glaring reminder
That I had been abandoned
A new chapter has begun
As I ink the space in love
A reminding message from deep inside
That I have life to offer and love resides
I am not covering the scar anymore
I am adding color and power
Forever reminding myself
That I am resilient despite all else

20.
Ron was the name at four I was assigned
Whose tenacity and exploration I relied
Of which I am now ready to resign
Roley was the name at four I was assigned
Whose caring and generous heart remains
Of which I am now ready to resign
Renee is the name and whom I want to be
Legally recognized and representing me
Severing that last bind and flying free

Riding played a huge role in my life
Providing opportunity, experiences, and finding of self
Forever grateful I will be as riding was a lullaby

Resiliency lifts me and helps me through
Bouncing me back from the slough
And that reminder is inked permanently in my skin

Fire burning as a fire was first step to the edge
        Burning buildings, fields, cars and houses
                I learned poise, respect and my courage
Fire burning as desire lit my caldron of self inspire
        For years it burned inside my soul
                Life energy lifting myself out of the hole
Fire burning very personal five years ago this day
        I searched into the world for something more
                That was when I met the Goddess Pele
Fire burning as an element newly self discovered
        Enhancing my yin with compassion
                As I strive for enlightenment
Fire burning on my skin, as the symbol is seared
        A visual image of family and intimacy shared
                And that reminder is singed permanently
        in my skin

R as Renee and Resiliency
        Fire as Family and Intimacy
                Both on my skin permanently
                        Thus my personal symbol shall be

21.
This moment I focus on each breath
        They are shallow and with effort
This moment all I can do is each small step
        Amidst an avalanche of requests
The burden of a property vision dissipating

I empty my accounts to sustain it
A speech next week to change bathroom policy
   And all I have is one word to speak audibly
A speech in two weeks abroad
   And all I can do is imagine
Increased visibility at work from the video
   Requires me to constantly be available
Relinquished responsibilities for leathers
   Puts me precariously in hands of others
Logistics and costs of traveling
   Put me afar and separating
As the only cadet without romance
   Reminds me of what's in my underpants
The permanent mark rings hallow
   As I 'will' resilience over my shadow

The constant use of pop culture
   Reminds me repeatedly of my child
A life of constant transience
   Leaves me living only in the edges
I am lost, I am floundering
   With no prospects I am stuck

"Your whole life has lead up to this point...
   let me take it from here."
     Seems silly and hollow
     though it's the only sliver I have now

And so ...

This moment I focus on each breath
   They are shallow and with effort

But they are breaths that take me forward
    And breaths that bring me grounding

This moment
    This minute
        This hour
            This week
                I focus on each breath

22.
I saw you,
    I watched you,
        I loved you

With a calm confidence
    With a strong center
        Without any shame
You proudly stood with audience
    Fully in the focus
        Fully present and proclaiming

I saw you,
    I watched you,
        I loved you

Less than a year ago
    You were still hiding in the shadows
        But there you are now out and lighted
August third was your first open ray
    And now you are seen every day
        More relaxed than ever in your space

I saw you,
       I watched you,
              I loved you

It's amazing to see you embracing your fluidity
       Really, freakin' outstanding
              Because you've important words to say
Standing feet firmly planted self-wide open
       You offered perspective and clarity
              Finding the power in vulnerability

I saw you,
       I watched you,
              I loved you

And yet a clear distinction is growing
       In reaction to the refocused attention
              In reaction to the accolades from others
Standing in your new found self-worth
       While grateful for the response
              You are not living for their praise

I see me,
       I watch me,
              I love me

23.
I see joy in my face
       utterly devoid of shame
I see a fluid being open
       without any guard in place

I see the multifaceted me
  all in one frame and celebrated
I see pure and willing vulnerability
  met with grace and understanding
I see confidence and ease
  relaxed to the fullest degree
As I begin to really settle
  into my leather center
This image captures beyond all other
  my journey of growth and power

24.
You were constructively vulnerable
You offered the team so much of yourself
Your personal stories were compelling
Your sharing educated them
You are full of powerful stuff
Your information needs to be shared deeper
You provided enlightenment
Your presentation made them think
You provided awareness of gender flexibility
You provided insight for safety
You offered learning on how you can be supported
You influenced immediate change
You showed courage
You provided a real conversation
You are more relaxed than ever
You are more confident than ever
You are an exceptional being
You asked them to call you Renee
You asked them to use your pronouns

You taught them how you want to be treated
You are creating your own culture of acceptance

25.
What are these feelings?
        Prickly against my skin
            Vibrating my heart
                Tickling my soul
                        Shortening my breath
                                Infusing adrenaline

How does this feel to create
        Connecting molecules into shape
How does this feel to inspire
        Teary-eyed heartfelt connections real
How does this feel to lead change
        Deeply moving and self-inspiring
How does this feel to be powerful
        Rooted to the core of the earth

What are these feelings?
        Personal power
            Personal path
                Personal purpose
                        Limitless and steady
                              Unbounded energy

How does this feel to be a "history maker"
        Confounding and unreal
How does this feel to be catapulted
        Flying into the depths of the universe
How does this feel to boundless

Beyond galaxies beyond dimension
How does this feel to be given a path
With focus and impact

What are these feelings?
Childlike in purity
Intense beyond measure
Infinite in possibilities
Hyper driven energy
Safe and protected

I feel like a star exploding
sending its energy
itself....myself
to billions of corners.

I feel I have energy that cannot be measured
Cannot be restrained
A stance that propels me
Sure footed with grace

26.
I have a rich tapestry of experiences
A being living an unusual life
Moving forward anyway
Willing to be vulnerable
Open even with the risks
Rejecting the fraud police
Thinking beyond binary
Holding steady on course
Youthful energy of I will

I am worthy to be heard
    I am worthy to be paid
        I am worthy because I am

27.
Where is the balance of being prideful,
    And of being boastful?
Where is the line between being humble,
    And puffing myself up?
When do I accept praise for my efforts,
    And when am I using it for my worth?
When can I hear "It's all because of you!"
    And allow an internal celebration?
When can I recognize the change I am causing,
    And be joyful and proud?
When can I recognize my personal power
    And accept my influence in the world?

I felt proud for a moment
    "gushing so full of pride"
I felt proud for a moment
    "proud that I am changing an entire culture"
It was fleeting and followed by confusion
    Despite wanting to roll around in it
When can I internalize this truth,
    That I am changing the world?
        I am
           I am
              I am
                I am

Changing the world

28.
A longing long resolved
Through the time of life
Having self nurtured as a child
I had released that foundational desire

Being attached to and loved
       I had longed for that latch
Being Held head in hand and fed
       I had yearned for that touch

A longing for freedom from the loss
Through the time with intentional focus
Having self propelled to forgiveness
I had released with purpose those demons

Being attached to and loved
       I had longed for that latch
Being Held head in hand and fed
       I had yearned for that touch

A longing I have quenched with reframing
Through time breathing peace and patience
Having witnessed exquisite motherhood
I had released and moved into joyfulness

A dry sponge soaks liquid into every corner
       Like the caring love and devotion of motherhood
A cracked earth becomes alive after a downpour
       Through her giving of her very self
A quenching of a thirst after a forever drought
       She reminds the world of what's important

An oasis in the desert of life is the liquid nurturing
        The two bonded in natural purity

Motherhood is being remodeled for me
        By many generous giving souls
Motherhood is being reframed for me
        As my gratitude bursts forth in tears...
                ...of joy
                        ...of love
                                ...of hope
                                        ...of peace
Now I look inward, and thank my self made mother
inside

29.
Bright and girlie
        With white laced trim

Petticoats ala' twirlie
        My joy fills to the brim

From the bonnet on my head
        To the mary janes on my feet
Earrings, cuffs and every thread
        All glorious shades of pink

Stockings over my knees
        with a little heel kick
shame is faded memories
        giggling through my lipstick

And now a dedicated bag
  To all of my sissy wear
And on the right is the pink flag
  As to the world I declare

I love to wear pink every day I can
  And share my little sissy side
I love how it feels to be free
  With loved ones I don't have to hide

30.
Why try,
  When I don't control the outcome
Why try,
  When goals don't mean anything
Why try,
  When all attempts are blocked
Why try,
  When I'm told I am "a nobody"
Why try,
  When the universe fucks me at every turn
Why try,
  When I am destined for aloneness
Why try,
  When intimacy passes me by like a ghost
Why try,
  To be ambitious if nothing I do matters
Why try,
  To inspire change if I am uninspiring
Why try,

A "path" is no different than "gods will"
Why try,
    To be clean when doping is rewarded
Why try,
    When I can never erase the pain of my youth
Why try,
    When the universe simply doesn't care

31.
Why try,
    When I don't control the outcome
        Because releasing attachment offers
    freedom
Why try,
    When goals don't mean anything
        Because there may be a different outcome
    I can't see
Why try,
    When all attempts are blocked
        Because I only need one to succeed

Why try,
    When I'm told I am "a nobody"
        Because this frees me from irrational
    pressures
Why try,
    When the universe fucks me at every turn
        Because it's not fucking you, it's helping
    you grow
Why try,
    When I am destined for aloneness
        Because you are built for community

Why try,
> When intimacy passes me by like a ghost
>> Because vulnerability allows for that
> intimacy

Why try,
> To be ambitious if nothing I do matters
>> Because it does matter, just don't tie
> yourself to it

Why try,
> To inspire change if I am uninspiring
>> Because you are inspiring simply by
> being you

Why try,
> A "path" is no different than "gods will"
>> Because I only see the tree for the forest

Why try,
> To be clean when doping is rewarded
>> Because I can rest in my personal
> integrity

Why try,
> When I can never erase the pain of my youth
>> Because that pain defined me and I
> celebrate that

Why try,
> When the universe simply doesn't care
>> Because I am of the universe, and I DO
> care

32.

> Climbing up to jump down, glimpsing over the
edge I saw no landing
> I wasn't pushed, I wasn't forced, but there was

only one way down

Like the bridge at the cove, my belly flipped and then I stepped out

Universe taking over increasing in speed propelling me now

With only that deciding step the path is no longer mine

I keep saying yes because there is no longer a way to say no

Radical changes are increasingly impactful and mind spinning

A complete global redesign of the bathroom experience

My message of fluidity being amplified beyond my voice

Convincing Digital to adjust the algorithm for fluid shopping

Convincing Brand to understand the need for a sport binder

Convincing Brand to understand the need for a sport gaff

Convincing retail to have staff to move beyond one gender approach

One on ones non-stop as strangers now approach daily

The influencer for an entire line focused on gender fluidity

Radical changes are increasingly impactful and mind spinning

I keep saying yes but I need the universe to hear me too

With only that deciding step the path needs to be

for me also
     Universe taking over and I can no longer keep up
life spinning out
     Like the bridge at the cove, the way down is long
and dangerous
     I wasn't pushed, I wasn't forced, but this is the
only path I have
     Climbing up to jump down, I need something to
land on that gives me hope...

...That.
     My.
          Experience.
             Matters.
                 Also.

33.
The wind blows and blows and blows
Through the valleys and over the groves

Pushing and bending and pulling
The trunks and cores are constantly moving

Maturing without a sheltered neighborhood
Growing a counter acting "reaction wood"

Stress is what makes a tree strong and healthy
Harsh forces develop internal stability

Reaching deep into mothers depths
Roots form and tangle creating strength

Without the wind hitting them daily
The center is weak and the spine is frail

Grown in the safe confines of a greenhouse
Plants and trees are weak and shallow

Adversity develops a strong internal core
Our challenges mold us into who we are

I have been buffeted and blown on plateaus alone
My resilience cannot be taken from me by anyone

34.
Sleeping in my own bed
Enjoying professional hair styling on the road
Lounging in my couch nest in the comfort of my home
Feeling the new possibilities of my abundant hair
Cooking for myself in my kitchen with my knives
Aging a craft cocktail in a barrel with my class
Receiving the orders of all lacy things pink
Expert comfort that is a salon mani and pedi
Refilling a bowl and a cookie with a fellow cadet
Easeful entry into the day with my espresso
Nurturing myself through the peaceful Oasis
Enthusiastic shame free self-pleasure
Experiencing the joy that are two energetic little ones

35.
A deeper dimension discovered
          With weight and gentle flow
Allowing space for multifaceted

Enjoying the new freedom of soul
It is a new symbol for my self-expression
        Pulling from the root of internal power
Feeling soft and full of decadent sensation
            Wafting gently as a field of wildflowers
Sinking deeper into my personality
        Beyond the confines of her or him
Calmly now accepting and embracing
        Limitless is my joyful spectrum
Sharing so often with sincere vulnerability
        Has been deeply self-affirming

Understanding how open can be my reality
        A new level of my center bringing

36.
From where does the inner strength come
        When so much pulls me so far
Without disintegrating like a crumb
        And not losing sight of my north star

Every day something new to say yes
        Opportunities finding me now
Every day new things adding to stress
        Strength keeping me afloat somehow

In those moments I feel like cracking
        I've become aware of the source
When emotional labor is overwhelming
        There exists a continual force

From one extreme of external aggression

As if they were sent to destroy
To the other extreme of internal acceptance
As if they were sent to buoy

I have discovered an inner source of power
Like a furnace that's always afire
It exists to my core radiant like a sunflower
Affirmation from others unrequired

From where does the inner strength come
Walking with gravitas through culture

Accessing this new tool to overcome
My strength is my growing leather center

37.
Moving through my world is different now
Moving through life if from my center
When I mindfully breathe and notice my power
When I allow that feeling to foster
Shifting how I physically walk
Shifting how I engage and talk

From slouching posture **TO** squared shoulders
From eyes cast down **TO** face up and proud
From shallow breath **TO** deep connected breathing
From feeling insecure **TO** a settled confidence
From hiding myself **TO** being fully open
From feeling like I don't belong **TO** creating my own
belonging
From glossy eyes **TO** eyes full of vibrant curiosity

From apologizing for who I am **TO** celebrating my
uniqueness
From hiding my hair **TO** letting it flow majestically
From hiding my nails **TO** proudly expressing color

When I breathe into my core, my center, my
actual power
I am settled, confident, calm and gentle
When I move through spaces from that place
I am kind and supportive to all even myself
Every step, then, has purpose and intention
As I notice and rev my internal nuclear reactor

38.
Who am I to love...
When I look past deeds
When I look past accolades

Who is the real me
Looking through the noise
Finding that quiet space

Answers hard to nail down
For I want to love myself or who I am
For I want to love myself not for what I do

So again, who am I to love...

Passionate, kind, curious
Full of so much to offer myself
Full of so much to offer others

Gentle, interesting, interested
Full of so much compassion
Full of so much energy

Powerful, brave, courageous
Full of genuine hope
Full of a desire to grow

I want to know more of me
As I become my own true lover
As I become my own true partner

39.
The unicorn on my chest pink and warming
Holding and accepting, being charged with intention
My love for me, everyone's love receiving

At the height of my vulnerability
Physically, emotionally and spiritually
I am opened fully, joyful love holding

Love to me
Love from me
Love for myself

Gazing with me, into me, through me
I feel your love deeply and finally
Your patient, kind, powerful...Love for me

At the height of my vulnerability
Physically, emotionally and spiritually
I am opened fully, joyful love holding

Love to me
Love from me
Love for myself

Resting on the unicorns glowing orb
Five fingers, connecting as one
We embrace through a higher orbit

At the height of my vulnerability
Physically, emotionally and spiritually
I am opened fully, joyful love holding

I don't need to test
I only need to trust
For love is abundant

40.
Want to love myself
Every morning every night
Leaving past behind

Want to fall backwards
Trusting once and ever for all
That I will be caught

Moving into love
Leaving old tapes behind me
Moving with all love

Reacting from love
Releasing response from fear
I am loveable

Relax into me
Hold vital intimacies
Sacred to my heart

Growing with learned tools
Allowing for possible hurt
Believing the best

Frequent Pause I will
In that moment I know well
Making a new choice

41.
When I am challenged to grow
    I am still loved
When I am offered feedback
    I am still loved
When I am provided space to reflect
    I am still loved
When expectations are high for me
    I am still loved
When I am physically apart
    I am still loved
When I am pushed to perform
    I am still loved
When I make a mistake
    I am still loved

When I am called in...even then
I am still loved

I am loved
I am loved
Because I am loveable

Because I am loveable
I can love myself
I love myself

42.
In mindful patience
Looking inward
One bird at a time
Veering into empathy
Each response considered
Moving with grace
Engaging from love

43.
Believe I am enough
Express gratitude within
Magically engage my inner child
Yearn for nothing
Own positivity
Welcome my uniqueness
Notice my self-worth
Lovingly caress my soul
Open up to vulnerability
Value all of me without judgment
Embrace old hurts gently
Release inner expectations

44.
Hiding and cowering in the dark corners of my soul
My inner child weeps and wants and patrols

Lashing out then into the dark retreating
A hyena leaving a trail of innocent beatings

Confined by chains fused and rusting
Unrelenting in pain and suffering

Pleading
Yearning
Hoping

I see you now, my inner child, and hold your pain
I comfort you, my inner child, and stroke your mane

Calling in the unicorn spirit guide to sit beside
To show how safe you are, and that love resides

We have a journey together through this storm
A focus on healing and loving and holding firm
    You are no longer abandoned
    You are no longer alone

I seek you with compassion to rise above
Break the chains and finally trust in love

I love you my inner child, I say aloud
You are so courageous, brave, and proud

Lets work together in one direction
You are released from duties of protection

Lets learn to play and prance with whimsy
Lighthearted, innocent, and freely

45.
  enjoYed
    prOtected
   secUre
    treAsured
 cheriRshed
   freE
       Sheltered
       Adored
    upliFted
    loved

46.
              You are wanted
             yOu are wanted
            yoU are wanted
           you Are wanted
          you aRe wanted
         you arE wanted
        you are Wanted
       you are wAnted
      you are waNted
     you are wanTed
    you are wantEd
   you are wanteD

47.

Innocent
faultless
wonderful
brave
guiltless
N
O
T
youthful
loveable
courageous
pure
free
clean
unbroken
blameless
innocent

48.

A beautiful feminine being ...
asking to be seen.
Shamed and forced inside ...
at the tender age of nine.
I see you fully now ...
you have lasted somehow.
I grieve our lost years ...
I embrace your tears ...
Unleashing you entirely now ...

Let's thrive in our power.

All of these things
          you "should not" be,
Are now traits I celebrate
          and fold into my being

          eMpathtic
    womanlY
      feelinG
        passIonate
        heaRtful
emotionaL
        forgIving
      humaNe
              Sensitive
      intuitIve
          unDerstanding
      vulnErable

50.
Months mindful planning
Inner kids gently engaged
I went in and did

51.
The water cleanses, rinsing, refreshing
Tiles sparkling with delicate gold flakes
Suit so feminine, breastly and empowering
Lights changing as I internally awake

Self-baptism for my inner spirit invigorating
As I reimagine being in a wanted womb
Four full days in deep intense reflection
More work to do but inside I'm abloom

52.

53.
Every race day when I was racing bicycles, my day
started the same. I would be woken up by our team
manager, and before rolling out of bed; I would review
again the race bible. The bible is a booklet that
summarizes every stage, how long, and most
importantly, the elevation changes.

Stage races tend to spend a fair amount of time in the
mountains, especially the Alps. The race profile always
looked foreboding, and the mornings were always a
somber affair knowing the suffering ahead. The
mountains were my kryptonite, because my job was
always to keep the group together until the climbs and
then somehow survive the climbs to race again the next
day.

When I was considering this work, the sensation I was feeling was eerily familiar, much like a morning stage. I knew what was coming, I could see it on paper and feel it in my legs. But most importantly, I couldn't stop time...it was going to happen, period.

I look at this bird, and the work it represents, and I know I am on this journey. I know I need to climb it and I can sense what that experience will be like, similar to those painful days in the Alps.

54.
Jagged like a row of teeth, unrelenting and steep
Day after day Alpe d'huez to Ventoux, time never sleeps

The long lead to the base, then unparalleled suffering and pain
Every morning filled with dread, and yet The Dragon must be slain

Each climb akin to a cave, while knowing the agony that awaits
As I shift from one bird to the next, I feel the same dreaded fate

Digging deep for energy, like coasting through a curve
Now time to take a deep breath, and lean into the next bird

Unknown how to approach this bird so devastating with reason

Whose like a vulture, constantly pecking at a festering lesion

The first and hardest step is to name it aloud and face it
I can't yet accept my dysfunction. I can't yet accept my penis.

Healing and accepting my everlasting wound
Embracing intimacy despite the side effects of doom

The vulture is the bird I now embrace, incomprehensibly brazen
Change into an eagle, I want to fly and swoop into true sexual freedom

55.
Untethered from the memories
Free from the toxic energies

The loss of a hopeful connection
Mourned but only for a fraction

No longer limiting me gravitationally
No longer a distraction emotionally

Fully released of all familial ties
Fully released of shameful binds

Forward now with positive momentum
No longer living with constant rejection

My orbit feels fresh and purified
My aura feels clear and energized

There is a big shift noticeably
Gratefully I am not his legacy

Free to soar Free to soar
Free to soar I am forever free to soar

56.
Crews numbering in trillions
In place at every neuron
Ready for my decision
No delay in construction

It is my decision to decide
Activating them to build
Nothing to do but decide
Then they build build build

Love response core build crew
        Building love response bridges
Love response enhancement crew
        Enhancing love response bridges
Love response gender reveal crew
        Revealing myself to my gender
Love response priority heart crew
        Responding with love to my heart
Love response priority penis crew
        Responding with love to my penis
Love response altered states crew
        Responding with love in any form

It is my decision to decide
Activating them to build
Nothing to do but decide
Then they build build build

Crews numbering in trillions
In place at every neuron
Ready for my decision
No delay in construction

57.
Comfortably strong
Sharing without a cower
Grounded in power

58.
Masturbating
Going well
Almost there
A scream cries out

Why do you hate me so?
     When I give you so much pleasure
Why must you shame me so?
     And not love me like I you

Shame takes over
Blunting my climax
Like a ruined orgasm
Much deeper an impact

The tip of my penis crying out
Dripping out white creamy tears
Showing much love for me
Not asking anything in return

59.
The root of my despair
   Is in the root of my being
It begs for love and acceptance
   But dangles, cold and receding
Its scarred visibly from abuse
   Its scarred invisibly by my thinking
It bears the brunt of my dysphoria
   Never feeling sexually attractive
It bears the brunt of my loneliness
   My self-confidence teetering
I have tip toed through life tentative
   Not with the swagger of BDE
Traumatized from years of humiliation
   I blame it for my life's failures

If only it functioned as intended

If only hard
If only big
If only beautiful

Yet

If I really love myself
      I must love all of myself
If I can love the root of my being
      I will be comfortable in aloneness
If I can be comfortable in aloneness
      I will be self assured
If I am self assured
      I will love my full self
If I love my full self
      I will love my penis
If I love my penis I
      will love all of myself
If I love all of myself
      I will respond to myself...

...with compassion
...with confidence
...with love

61.
The long temporary blindness is clearing
I can see now, it's a portal to my universe
I can see now, there is more than a phallus
I can see now, I'm inviting you in to my being

      Come fly with me, through limitless passion
Touching my penis is reaching into my expanse
      Come fly with me, and we will travel
Touching my penis is a journey you want to chance

As I remove my covering, opening myself to you for the first
My penis is the key, play with it with me, and lets fly free
Flinging effortlessly through the magellanic cloud
Melding physical and spiritual, unconstrained from gravity

      Come fly with me, through limitless passion
Touching my penis is reaching into my expanse
      Come fly with me, and we will travel
Touching my penis is a journey you want to chance

A passion of purity and connection, joy and pleasure
The soft touch, lips to skin, lingering to savor every sense, every taste
Love holds us safe in the softness of clouds the size of ten galaxies
I'm clearing the blocks in my sexual relationship to myself and you

      Come fly with me, through limitless passion
Touching my penis is reaching into my expanse
      Come fly with me, and we will travel
Touching my penis is a journey you want to chance

I have the creative power of the universe at my genitals
Sexual energy, life force energy, creative energy are the same
Newly started is the fire in my cauldron of desire

Harnessing the power of my pelvis to unleash into the
world

62.
An embrace without constructs
I see no bounds or frontiers
I give to you from my core
Licentiously exploring

Plucking nerves like a banjo
Merging frequencies deeply wide
Where two flames can burst
Body soul safe no need to hide

My limitless taste fascination
Lifting open access to all realms
Syncing our flame to flame
Without shame or frowns!

For I am here for you
Yes, differently functioned
For I am here with you
Bridging our Twin Flames
Come intersect with me
Energy fields double fusing
Come converge with me
Light years of love flourishing

For I am not your typical
I am not your traditional

I embrace now my uniqueness
I thirst to be explored

I invite you
      into my life force
I invite you
      into mirroring souls

63.
You can fly me, I'll let you, if you fly me, you GET to
When you touch me, I fly, YOU fly ME
Clime on!
Magic carpet is me and you get to have a spree
I beckon you on, in, into on, and with
Like a conductor on a happy train to the sea
I load you on
Choose your berth carefully in me, with me

You GET to

You can fly me, I'll let you, if you fly me, you GET to
Tug me around your world and share it with me
Your passions, joys, pains, let me soak you in
With a crave of curiosity and glee!
Thirsting for you, frequency matching!
Let me flip over, allow me the reigns, control
I'll fling you along new byways
Within your OWN soul!! Let me!

You GET to

You can fly me, I'll let you, If I fly you, YOU get to

Dip your lips softly into my surface
Breaking gently the protective glass sheen
Slowly clearing I, like magnifying exposing
So deep so thick so circled and ...
... and ... and available
to you, only you, in this moment
My universe is so fascinating and profound
I so...so... so want to show you around!
Every neuron anew together we attach

You GET to

You can fly me, I'll let you, If you dive into me, YOU get to
For I am to be cherished
My being celebrated
Together! As one, even for a moment
We can ride a wave
Or two ... or three, three trillion!
I offer a journey, rare, complex, me
I offer me, joyfully
I am a treat, consume me, ravenously!
You get to, I'll let you! I'll let YOU, let I will

You GET to

64.
Meet me in vulnerability
        It is safe. I am safe.
Meet me in connectivity
        Together we are safe

And in that safety
      We can release
In that safety
      We can climb
          Each other, in myself

Each molecule of our being intersect
      And for that short time
glides into sunsets of pleasure
        Of lust ... Of exploration ... Of taboo

I / We don't need anyone else, we are ourselves...
...Enough!

Together combined
      I can offer me masculinity
         For I am a HE
Together combined
      I can offer femininity
         For I am a SHE
Together combined
      I can offer me infinite blends
         For I am a THEY

Energies in passion
      Aggressively owning and fucking
Energies in sensuality
      Softly exploring touch and love
Energies in empathy
      I hold them all, for me, for you, for us

For I am meeting myself in vulnerability

Myself, with myself, is the height of intimacy
For I am connecting with myself holistically
To myself, for myself, is the height of love

Outside of me I welcome you
Inside
Rarely do I offer
I do now
Witness with me, me loving me

65.
While alone I remain whole in communion with myself
My fingers an extension of energy and sensation
Guiding body into bliss with no need for another
Particles of my physical being merging, lips luscious
Lines becoming blurred and ultimately needless

I am a spiritual entity
Navigating the physical realm
In a borrowed body

In the soft states, all too common and real
When my soul steeps in sadness
I imagine it curling in on itself, finally disappearing

... inward
... caving
... morphing
... gendering

In hard states my lust and pleasures are uninhibited
I caress and hold in wonder this engorged nerve
My soul, even in this joy, cries out to be witnessed

The exploration of self-sensuality, in bliss with myself
The integration of self-sensuality with other selves,
within and without
The interaction of self-sensuality with nature, physical
and universal

In union with myself ... my body ... my soul ... my star
beings
Freely exploring space and time with little constraint
Physical body but a limited tool for my spirit
Moving beyond self pleasure into self-sensuality
I float above ... and embrace ... my own needs

66.
Through the brambles, thorns dense. Impassable
Keep ON!
Your skin scratches, wounding, with pointed barbs
it is worth it, though you cant see it, wouldn't know it
the path grown o'er
only a small fraction, of me, now secret no more!

I implore you, invite you, desire you,
to find it, find me, view inside me beyond all veils
through all walls.
Peonies dancing with their skirts of pink petalcoats
all of their layers pufting out, over gentle roley hills

willow trees offer you their switches like whips

next to a yellow waterfall, misting, coating, I thirst for
dream for
as boulders of chocolate are ripe for biting, tasty and
warm
bitter in richness, earthy and strong

Slippery slides you can glide into caves deep and wide
openings beckoning you, hungry to pull you in
curvy smooth solid stems exploding like spikes into the
ground
with silky cobwebs like lace seduce you, me, more me

vines crawling wrapping, holding
Clown Fish follow her with Marsh Harriers patrolling
above
as they shift and evolve into all
I too am all. you can see all, as I open me

Fenceless farms dot the edges, hidden from direct view
I'll take you there if you let me, please say yes...let's go!
Eyes connecting as no words, panting matching
Beasts connecting on a different plane
but with me the same, equal are they

Tree stumps as presenting stools, formed and fitted
For me, to present, me presenting to you
I am ready, always, wanting always
Allow me ... to present

The divine liquid, crimson and bold, from my skin seeps
with flow
As the twills prick and poke

I am here, for you, for us
Glorious and free from the core to beyond the reaches of
the universe
unmanicured, wild, waiting for your touch, your vision
you have arrived

67.
A voice alone, speaking into a void
Seemingly unnoticed or understood
Yet opening myself for all to see
What did all of it really mean?

A Valiant Voice

Clinging to a hope for empathy
For the arch of acceptance to lean bending...
...to me, viewed differently for my authenticity
As my voice grew, it became more costly

A Valiant Voice

And then, revealed, I had been seen...
...felt, heard, appreciated, and embraced
Announced with my chosen name
Recognized as my inner gender

A Valiant Voice

Seen as the woman I feel inside
By the women I work with outside
Seen as daring, fearless, courageous

By acting with bravery and boldness

A Valiant Voice

Clearly a moment to dedicate
But not to dwell or overthink
Clearly a moment to celebrate
Feeling what it means to be thanked

A Valiant Voice

68.
She so soft and silky, warm, open, needing
Curves smooth, a deep craving for penetration
She is bending, over, hips gently gesturing
A willingness, a wantonness, gasping for him

He observes and gives her space to reveal
To revel, to work herself up for him, to him
He enjoys feeling his hardness, existing there
Throbbing, untouched, waiting and glorious

She beckons with her mind her soul her essence
Expanding her energy as confidence builds
She takes him all in, skin melting into skin
Connecting passion, connecting tissues

He gazes in awe, her beauty new, seen, valued
Confidence of his own self, flourishing, visible
He is aroused by this beautiful creature
Syncing with her he thrusts, taking, penetrating

They ride together, joined into one energy
Mingling, writhing, accepting, elevated craving
They hold the other, giving all to, and taking all
Flying through the nebulas in orgasmic waves

They are one, He is she, She is he
One physical container holding both
But free to be all within as spirits
Colliding, loving, holding both. One.

69. Part One
A lifetime of disgrace
Never without dread
Always wanting it dead

Embarrassment consuming
Isolating my being
To save the revealing

In a moment it all changed
Gratefully surprised
Forever now resides

In my life for the first time
It felt like mine
Sexy and pure

In my mind for the first time
I see it with pride
Perfectly sublime

In my heart for the first time
I am overjoyed by how pretty
Stunned by no shame

In awe as I stood forward
My reflection gazed back
Never ever had I felt that

And now I did, as I glowed
Taking in its cuteness
Resplendently perfect

Sissy clitty in pink ribbon and bow
Dressed in flexible chastity
I finally felt whole

Matching my pink shoes
Body hairless
Naked now known

Now I can reflect
Accept me with my head
No longer any dread

For the first moment ever
I embraced myself fully
And...for once...I felt whole

69. Part Two
Come play with me, it beckons

I beckon, you, me, we
Small and dainty, pink and safe
It brings me joy in this moment
I want to share it with you
I want to dance and prance and bounce with joy
And let you in
Lets dive as if into a pool of flower petals
My full self actualized and loved
Join me Laugh and tease and lead me around
With the ribbon extended into your hand controlling
For I finally feel free, without shame
Feeling me without disgrace
Admiring myself
Letting the gift of me in, to me, to you, to we

70.
Celebrating fluidity within me, yes!
Appreciating all of that growth
Accepting I've been a girl inside
How do I want her shown?

Squeezing into a crossroads
Lingering near the neck
Struggling with unknowns
Which direction will it tip

Part becomes whole
Transitions into infinity
Another life to live
Fully expressing femininity

Building momentum
Forward and through
Can I? Do I? Will I?
Or am I too matured?

I will feel and be a different me
Or all the sames' before?
What is holding me back
Is it scorn I fear or more?

Ultimately it's me seeing me
For who I have always felt to be
The question isn't am I?
Is it only about my courage?

Do I transition?
Do I express whom I feel inside?
Do I share her with the world?
Do I keep her safe in mind?

71. Part One
I see a girl, me, in the mirror
Tentatively self-accepting
I grapple with feeling inferior
Not fully seeing, I am actually her

My fingertips graze the glass
Reaching to her desperately
As hers meets mine reflecting
Fingerprints softly corresponding

And then gone, fleetingly
As the brunt face of reality
No longer back reflecting
Vacant, blank and empty

Refocusing on the silvering
Editing out my physical being
Only them do I choose to see
Fabric that reflects my genderality

Vampire like from reflection secreting
On days I can muster to look and see
My intricately constructed vision of me
Is shattered leaving me cold, and weeping

I have built a view of myself for myself
As a means of self acceptance and love
The slightest reflection from a mirror
Evaporates that construct into dysphoria

Not fully seeing, I am actually her
I grapple with feeling inferior
Tentatively self-accepting
I see a girl, me, in the mirror

71. Part Two
    Window
   s**H**iny car
  gl**A**sses
   s**T**ubble
how **I** pee
    Shoulders
  leg**A**l name
   My voice
cloth**I**ng
  d**R**ivers license
finge**R**s
  z**O**om
othe**R**s eyes

Integration
embracing my full self

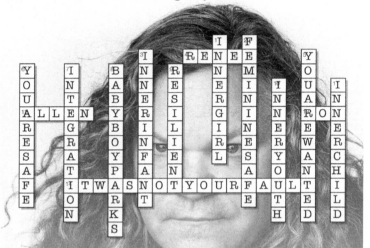

ACROSS

4 me in my full integrated power. Confident, secure, worthy, loved and loving.

12 a short part of you I welcome in

13 a large part of you who is loved

14 a release of shame and the ability to look beyond being a victim into a sense of appreciation and gratitude for the being you have become because of your life experience

DOWN

1 my feminine side who is melding together with all of me shifting and shaping

2 that which you can be expressively without shame

3 my innocent infant reaching out with connecting energy

5 a self confidence that you are wanted and worthy because of who you are not what you do

6 understanding that while you have been hurt, you are safe to express yourself and to respond out of love

7 my desire to unify my multi faceted self and integrate all of my life experiences in a positive way

8 new you. Strong you.

9 radiating through my youthful smile, this is comforting side of me is permanently on my wrist

10 resilient and powerful youth who is uniting with my full self bringing that youthful joy

11 that tender child that is merging with my greater self

Made in the USA
Las Vegas, NV
18 November 2020